Empathy IS YOUR SUPERPOWER

Empathy IS YOUR SUPER POWER

A Book About Understanding the Feelings of Others

WRITTEN BY
Cori Bussolari, PsyD

ILLUSTRATED BY
Zach Grzeszkowiak

ROCKRIDGE
PRESS

For general information on our other products and services or to obtain technical support, please contact our Customer Care Department within the United States at (866) 744-2665, or outside the United States at (510) 253-0500.

Rockridge Press publishes its books in a variety of electronic and print formats. Some content that appears in print may not be available in electronic books, and vice versa.

Interior and Cover Designer: Angie Chu
Art Producer: Sue Bischofberger
Editor: Lori Tenny
Production Editor: Mia Moran

Illustration © 2020 Zach Grzeszkowiak

ISBN: Print 978-1-64739-358-8 | eBook 978-1-64739-359-5

R0

Printed in China

This book is dedicated to my parents,
two of the most caring and loving models of
empathy a person could have had.

We are all born with superpowers!

Emma and Emmanuel's superpower
is called empathy.

Empathy is an awesome superpower.
With a little bit of curiosity, imagination, and
kindness, we can all have empathy, too.

Have you ever seen a friend feel so sad about something that you felt sad, too?

Then you've already started building your empathy superpower.

Empathy means understanding and caring about someone else's feelings and wanting to lend a helping hand.

Ask yourself two questions:

"How would I feel if that happened to me?"

"What would make me feel better?"

Astros
00:00
Nets
54
65
QTR:4
Astros
8

Empathy is one of your most important superpowers!

When you use it, you show kindness to others. You help them feel better because they know someone understands and cares about them.

How do you know when someone is being a good friend?

Can you remember when you were being a good friend?

How do you think your behavior made your friend feel?

Emma first learned about empathy one day when she was not feeling well.

She was sad, and her mom came to comfort her.

Even though her mom wasn't sick, she could imagine how Emma felt. She wanted to take care of her and help her feel better.

Can you remember a time when you were feeling sad or sick and someone showed you they cared about you?

What do you do to show someone that you care about them?

We all have our own feelings.

Sometimes you may feel happy or excited.
Other times, you could feel sad, scared, or angry.
Sometimes, you might want to tell other people
how you feel.

When you have an empathy superpower,
other people might want to tell you how they feel,
too, because they know you will be kind.

How can you tell how someone else is feeling?

What does your face look like when you have different feelings?
Look in the mirror to find out!

Emma and Emmanuel know that being human is beautiful. We all have feelings. And we are all born with the ability to show others we understand and care about them.

They practice using their empathy superpower
every day, just like you can. Let's see how!

Emmanuel and his brother Joshua were having fun riding their bikes. Suddenly, Joshua fell down!

His knee was scraped, and he started crying.
Emmanuel saw that Joshua was hurt.
He ran over to Joshua, asked how he could help,
and told him that it was going to be okay.

How did Emmanuel practice his empathy superpower?

What are some things you could have said to Joshua if you were with him?

Emma saw a group of girls making fun of her friend Ming's shoes. Emma could imagine how sad Ming felt.

Emma wanted Ming to feel better.
She said to her, "Let's each wear one of each other's shoes for the rest of the day!"

How did Emma practice her empathy superpower?

Have you ever seen someone being bullied? How did that make you feel?

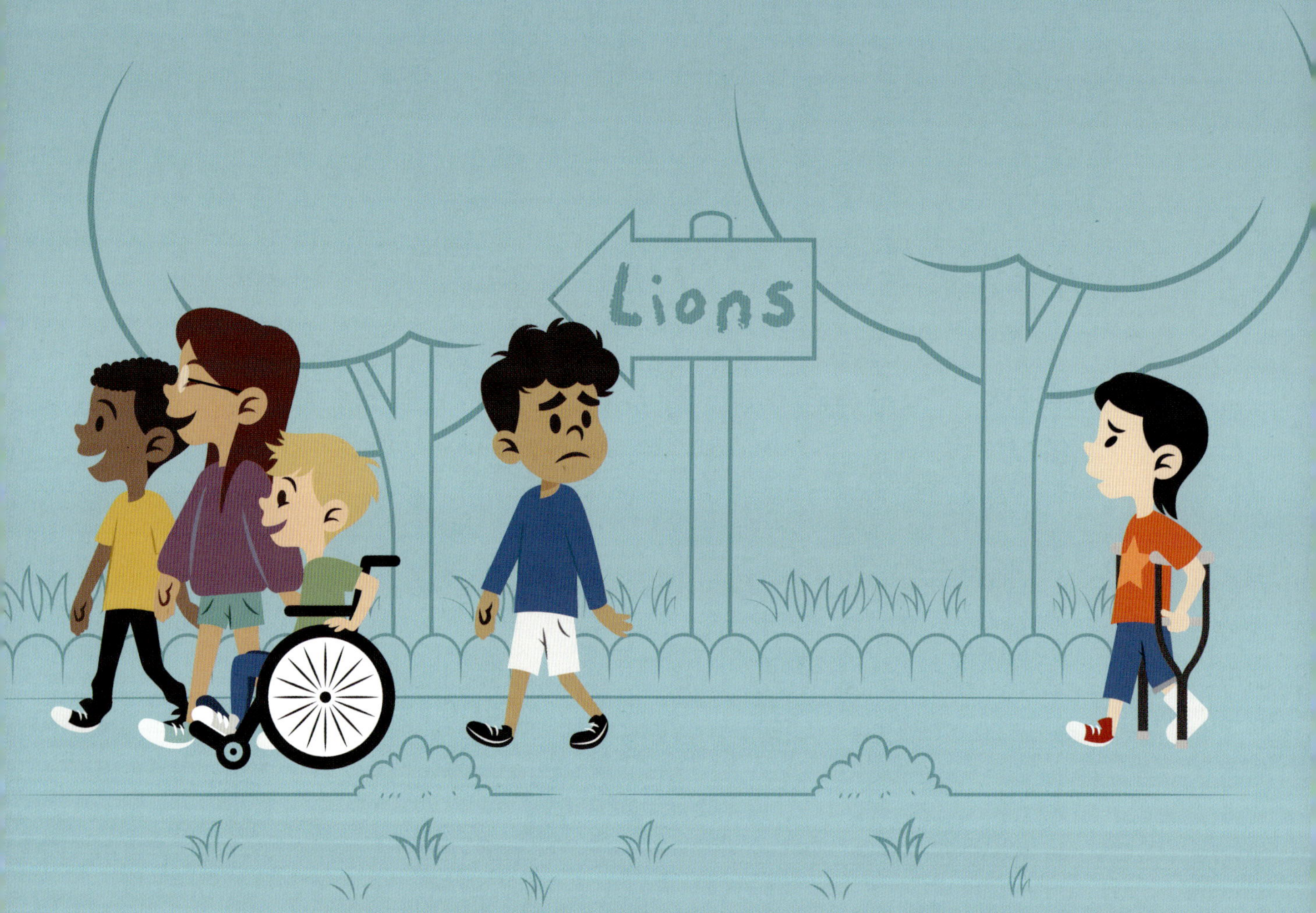

Emmanuel's class went on a trip to the zoo.
Emmanuel noticed that Darren, who had broken his ankle,
was struggling to keep up.

Emmanuel slowed down to walk with Darren. He said, "Let's take our time and look at all the animals."

How did Emmanuel use his empathy superpower?

How would you feel if you were Darren?

Alia is a new girl in school who doesn't speak English very well. Alia sat by herself every day during recess.

Emma thought Alia might feel lonely. She asked, "Do you want to play hopscotch with me?"

How did Emma use her empathy superpower?

Did you ever help someone who was new to your school or neighborhood? What did you do?

Emmanuel brought his favorite meal to school for lunch.
He saw that Luke had only a bag of chips.
Emmanuel imagined that he would still be hungry
if that was all he had to eat.

He said to Luke, "I'm not that hungry. Will you share this with me?"

How did Emmanuel use his empathy superpower?

Have you ever shared something? How did that make you feel?

Emma was at the amusement park with her family.
She loved to go on all the rides, even the scary ones!

Emma's sister, Leyla, started crying.
She wanted to go on the big-kid rides,
but she was too young.

Emma said to Leyla, "Don't worry. We can go on the smaller rides together. Sometimes those are the best ones!"

How did Emma use her empathy superpower?

Have you ever been left out because you were too young or too small? How did that make you feel?

It was a beautiful day, and Emmanuel could hear kids playing outside. "Why don't you go with them and have fun?" his grandpa asked.

Emmanuel knew his grandpa was not feeling well. He said, "I would rather stay here with you, Grandpa. I want to hear more stories about when you were my age!"

How did Emmanuel use his empathy superpower?

What are some ways that you show your friends and family that you care about them?

Emmanuel is in Zahra's reading group at school.

Zahra told Emmanuel that she doesn't like to read out loud because she makes mistakes.

Emmanuel said, "If you want, you can practice your reading with me! We can make mistakes together."

How did Emmanuel use his empathy superpower?

What are some things you would like someone to say to you when you make a mistake?

Emma and her brother Rudy were so excited.
They were going to the animal shelter to adopt a dog!

After meeting all the dogs, Emma said she wanted to adopt the big dog with the scruffy hair. Rudy said, "No way! He's the ugliest dog."

Emma asked Rudy to imagine what the dog might be feeling. She said, "He is sweet and has been at the shelter the longest. I can tell that he's sad and needs a good home."

How did Emma use her empathy superpower?

Why did Emma want this specific dog?

Emma and Emmanuel realized that empathy can be contagious!

Emmanuel saw Zahra helping someone with math.
Emma spotted Rudy including someone in a game.
Ming was giving a box of tissues to someone who was crying.

If you show others that you understand and care about how they feel, they do the same for someone else. You set a good example for everyone when you use your empathy superpower!

What does it mean to say that empathy is contagious?

How do you think you can use your empathy superpower?

for **PARENTS, EDUCATORS,** *and* **CAREGIVERS**

Empathy Superpower Practice!

Tips and Activities to Help Kids Cultivate Kindness, Compassion, and Consideration for Others

Empathy is truly a superpower. It is our ability to understand and care about how someone else is feeling, even if we aren't feeling the same way. Empathy is not only important for the development of healthy social relationships and qualities such as caring and kindness, but it also breeds courage, compassion, and, consequently, more life satisfaction. Equipped with empathy, we are better able to cultivate a connectedness with humanity and have the skills to participate positively in society. It is one of the most important traits we can nurture within children.

Empathy must be modeled, practiced, and strengthened, just like a muscle. Children first learn about empathy when they watch the actions of the important adults in their lives. They also learn about empathy from peers, such as Emma and Emmanuel, the superheroes of empathy in this book.

Empathy begins when we model what it looks like to put ourselves in someone else's shoes, even though it can be different from what we are experiencing. This is something that our children can learn and practice every day.

The activities in this section give parents, educators, and caregivers a chance to model the principles of empathy, then have their children put these principles into practice.

Through these activities, we can bring out an empathy superpower in everyone!

Celebration Ritual

For your birthday or another special occasion, visit a facility where you can be of service to others, such as a homeless shelter or an animal shelter. Bring your child along to help. Talk to your child about how it makes you feel to do something for other people on a day that is special to you. Talk about how you feel when you show someone you care about them.

Superpower Practice!

Have your child choose a service project that they want to do. While doing it, ask them about their feelings. Talk about how you feel watching them make this kind gesture.

Discussion Questions

Why do you think that I wanted to help people or animals out when I could have spent the day doing something else?

How do you think these people or animals feel?

Why do you think we should care about how these people or animals feel?

Why is the service project you chose for your superpower practice important to you?

How Are They Feeling?

When you are at a park or restaurant with your child, try to discern how people around you are feeling and talk about this with your child. For example, "I think that the man in the red shirt is feeling happy because he is smiling," or, "That girl with the blue hat looks sad because she has tears in her eyes. She also just dropped her ice cream." Ask your child to talk about the feelings they can observe in other people as well.

Superpower Practice!

Have your child look at magazine photographs and ask them to tell you what is happening in the scene and how they think the people in it are feeling. You can also pick a feeling and have your child cut out pictures that reflect it. Alternatively, while watching movies together, ask your child to talk about the way the characters are feeling.

Discussion Questions

What do you think is happening in this scene?

How are each of these people feeling?

Why do you think they are feeling this way?

What might have happened before this picture was taken?

If you were to use your empathy superpower for one person in this picture, what would you say or do?

Feelings Charades

With another adult as your partner, choose a feeling (but don't tell your child) and act it out without using any words. Have your adult partner try to guess what the feeling is in front of your child. When they guess correctly, have your partner talk about why they guessed that feeling.

Superpower Practice!

Have your child think of a feeling. Tell them to act it out without using words, just like you did. Guess what feeling your child is trying to convey. If you guess correctly, discuss what facial and body language cues helped. If you guessed incorrectly, discuss what your child was trying to show versus how it appeared. Then switch roles.

Discussion Questions

How did you know what feeling I was acting out?

Can you make the same feeling with your face?

Is it sometimes hard to tell when people are feeling this way?

Was there anything else I could have done to make this easier?

If you were acting out this feeling, how would you have done it?

Why do you think it is important to know how people are feeling?

Kindness Wall

Designate a portion of a wall in your house or at school as the Kindness Wall and cover it completely with paper that you can write or draw on. Every time you see your child do something kind, whether it's big or small, point it out and write it on the wall. You can even use stickers and stars! Tell them how it makes you feel when they do something kind for you and when you see them do something kind for others.

Superpower Practice!

Ask your child to write or draw on the Kindness Wall every time they see someone do something kind for a person in need. They can also write or draw when someone else has been kind to them. When you can, point out acts of kindness when your child doesn't notice.

Discussion Questions

What does it feel like to do something kind for someone?

How does it feel when someone tells you that they noticed that you did something nice?

Why do you think we should do kind things for others? If the child says something like, "Because it is nice to do that," talk about what makes it nice for the other person and for your child.

Do you think that people feel good after doing something kind, even if no one knows they did it?

My Heroes

Bring up a situation in which other people or animals need our help (such as homelessness, discrimination, animal cruelty, antisemitism, racism, etc.). Discuss what it means and how it looks in the world in a way that your child will understand. If possible, check in with your child's school to see if they are doing anything like this so you can work on it at home as well. Together, research and learn about the work that people in your community are doing to change the world and make it better. If possible, go and meet them. You can even choose people you know who are giving back in impactful ways, such as family members or friends. Talk about the qualities that make them so empathic and caring. Ask your child why they think these people are empathy superheroes.

Superpower Practice!

Have your child draw a picture of an empathy superhero they met or learned about. Then, ask them to think of something they would like to do to make the world a better place or help others in need. Have them draw a self-portrait of themselves acting as an empathy superhero.

Discussion Questions

Tell me about your empathy superheroes.

Why are they your empathy superheroes?

How do they make others feel?

How do they help the world?

Tell me about your empathy superpower.

How do you practice your empathy superpower?

How would you like to use your empathy superpower when you get older?

Listening Circle: Model Active Listening

Ask your child to tell you about something that happened to them that day. Keep eye contact and don't ask any questions other than to cue them to tell you more. When they are done, say, "This is what I heard you say," and repeat as much back as possible. Explain that when we really listen to what people say to us, it shows them that we care about them. When we fully listen and pay attention to others, we are better able to respond in a helpful and kind way.

Superpower Practice!

Set up a designated "listening circle" time each day or week for 15 minutes. The more people you can get, the better. Help your child practice listening to everyone's stories and re-telling as much as possible.

Discussion Questions

How did you show that you were listening?

How do you imagine it made me feel?

Why do you think listening is part of having an empathy superpower?

Who listens to you the best?

How do you feel when that happens?

Stop-Think-Choose-Do

Teach your child to problem-solve situations rather than act impulsively. This will help them read cues in situations as they get older. It will also help them determine a helpful and empathic response. Teach them to "Stop" and determine what the problem is, "Think" and brainstorm about what another person might be experiencing, "Choose" an empathic response, and "Do" something helpful. Use something that happens when you are both together to facilitate this.

Superpower Practice!

Create some fictional scenarios that your child could potentially experience. For example, "You heard that your good friend was calling another friend a nickname they didn't like behind their back." Go through the Stop-Think-Choose-Do steps to help your child brainstorm empathic solutions.

Discussion Questions

What is happening in this situation?

How would you feel?

Why do you think you would feel this way?

What are some helpful and kind things you could do?

Which one is the best one?

Resources

TeachHeart.org/about
Teach Heart is a nonprofit that offers free services to public school districts to help develop compassionate and socially conscious youth.

Tolerance.org
Teaching Tolerance's programs provide free resources for educators and practitioners who work with youth to support their active participation in social justice and anti-bias activities.

DesignForChange.us
Design for Change provides educational materials to support youth in developing empathy and putting it into social action.

ParentToolkit.com
The Parent Toolkit is a free resource for parents regarding all aspects of social and emotional development.

GreaterGood.Berkeley.edu
Greater Good Magazine provides free resources and evidence-based information on empathy and other skills such as compassion, gratitude, and happiness.

ParentingScience.com
Parenting Science is a free website for parents, educators, and practitioners on all aspects of child development.

Us.RootsofEmpathy.org
Roots of Empathy offers educators empathy-based programs for children.

StartEmpathy.org
Start Empathy is an initiative to help create a more empathic society.

EmpathyLab.uk
Empathy Lab provides opportunities to build children's empathy through literature.

Acknowledgments

At the beginning of each semester, I tell my students that being a therapist is one of the most awesome gigs they could have chosen. I truly believe this! I am continuously grateful to the beautiful people (both students and clients) who let me into their lives every day so that I can be of service to them in some capacity. To my husband, Ray, who takes care of so many things for me: I am forever indebted to you for your love and kindness, always. Because of you, I got to spend my time writing this sweet children's book. And to my (sort of) furry animals, whose love and (what I can only describe as) empathy make all the challenging times so much easier. Last, a great big thank you to my editor, Lori Tenny, who encouraged me to do something I have never done before—become a children's book author!

About the Author

Cori Bussolari, PsyD, is an associate professor in the Department of Counseling Psychology at the University of San Francisco in San Francisco, California, where she teaches and trains master's students to become therapists. She is also a licensed psychologist (CA PSY20755) and a credentialed school psychologist working in private practice in San Francisco. Dr. Bussolari has worked in hospital, clinic, and educational settings throughout her career. She is passionate about supporting people experiencing grief, trauma, and chronic illness, and about helping people develop positive coping skills, such as self-compassion, when faced with significant life transitions. She deeply believes that, with mental health access, we all have the capacity to discover our inherent strengths and feel better. Her research is currently in the area of disenfranchised grief, specifically companion animal loss. She lives in Northern California with her husband, dog, and hairless cat.

About the Illustrator

Zach Grzeszkowiak is a graphic designer and illustrator originally from the Chicagoland area. He creates both digital and printed marketing materials like logos, infographics, and catalogs. In addition to his responsibilities as a designer, Zach also enjoys illustrating, animating, and sculpting colorful and exciting characters. Some of his favorite things to draw are animals and spooky creatures. He is constantly improving his skill set by drawing every day and experimenting with new mediums to work with. His favorite types of projects to work on involve educating, storytelling, and helping a cause. To him, there's nothing quite as rewarding as using your talents and strengths to help a cause that you care deeply about.